To Opal & Fred
May Grandpa's book
be a delightful tonic
for both of you!

Karen Ritchler

Sugar *for* Hiccups

Grandpa's notes on health, happiness
and a comfortable pair of shoes

Edited by Karen and Lance Ritchlin

Sugar *for* Hiccups

ISBN 0-9714162-0-6
Library of Congress Control Number: 2001119146

A Celtic Fires© ® book
Published by R-Star Productions, Inc.
P.O. Box 13
Littleton, CO 80160

Production design by Carol Magin Stearns
Cover photo by Richard Garcia

The editors gratefully acknowledge the contributions and cooperation of the following persons:

Grandpa's daughters, Phyllis Gruda and Ines Wilson

The family of Grandpa Al Brandt

Carolyn Ritchlin

Joyce Williams

About Grandpa

For Grandpa Al Brandt (1906–1979), a pocket notebook was his constant companion. In this notebook, he jotted down his life — the best advice, tastiest recipes, funniest jokes, most effective cleaning and gardening methods, shrewdest tips on money management and answers to some of life's most confounding riddles.

Like many people of his generation, he endured a couple of world wars, the Great Depression and the loss of loved ones, including his wife, Mary. The entries to his journals reflect these influences. From humble beginnings, he developed a knack for getting the most out of sparse resources. As Grandpa put it, "Make it do or do without." His notebooks are a treasure trove of little-known uses for vinegar and the cleaning and medicinal properties of baking soda. His notes on gardening reflect his love of simple beauty. But often, his interest in herbology found practical applications in a world before HMOs.

Although much of what he recorded is still practical for readers, Grandpa's journals also paint a picture of a beloved character. He was a dapper man, rarely seen in public without his hat. Kind of spirit but curmudgeonly in demeanor, Grandpa Brandt was fond of personalizing his journal entries with wry asides that bring this character to life. "Cranberry juice good for kidneys — not mine," he notes sourly.

His is a rare legacy, a stream-of-consciousness view of the world that takes nothing for granted. It is as if he observed every detail of life around him and said, "This is important. I'm going to write this down!"

May all our lives be that noteworthy.

Karen and Lance Ritchlin

Warning

The medical, diagnostic, dietary and herbal suggestions in this book are presented for their humorous and nostalgic content only and should not be construed as accurate or safe. Consult a doctor before using or adapting any of the medical methods, tonics or remedies herein.

Readers should acquaint themselves with — and abide by — all applicable local, state and federal laws and regulations pertaining to the acquisition, use, storage and disposal of chemicals and substances mentioned in this book. Cleaning tips have not been tested and could cause damage to fabrics and other materials or pose health risks.

The editors assume no liability for any danged fool who ignores common sense and poisons himself or puts somebody's eye out.

Table of Contents

Grandpa's Remedies

In children, the power of suggestion will remove warts and some adults.

People should sleep north and south.

Cranberry juice good for kidneys — not mine. Radish will dissolve gallstones. Paprika for infection.

A flax seed will remove small articles in eye.

A tablespoon of vinegar to a cup of water and rinse hair for itchy scalp.

If watchband causes sores from perspiration, put roll-on deodorant on wrists.

To get swelling to go down, soak cloth in a mixture of vinegar and salt and apply to where skin is unbroken. In ten minutes it will disappear.

A glass of orange juice or half of a green pepper will give you enough vitamin C for one day, 45 mg.

Arthritic hands: stick a pen or pencil through a large raw potato, which can be easily and painlessly grasped by an arthritic hand.

Beauty facial to remove pimples — every night at bedtime, work a big lather with pure Castile soap, spread all over face and let dry ten minutes, then brush the lather all over face in a gentle, circular movement to remove blackheads with soft brush, then remove all lather with water, then cold water, then pat on witch hazel with cotton ball. Your face will tingle and feel clean.

Tie four knots in a string and bury it in the ground. Within two weeks the warts will disappear — they are a virus.

Word to those suffering from asthma and hay fever: try to breathe through your nose. Ragweed pollen sprayed into nasal passage of hay fever victims does not trigger attacks; only those who breathe through their mouths are the ones who suffer.

Sugar for hiccups. One dry teaspoon of white granulated sugar, swallow. Works 50% of time.

Diarrhea: eat bananas, ripe, good. Carrot soup, puree or mash vegetable to a pulp. Pulp of ripe apples, no skin or core, no sweetening or spices. Oriental tea because it has tannic acid. Carob powder known as Saint John's. Bread — too much can cause constipation.

To remove sliver, fill pop bottle with hot water, hold over sliver, steam will soften so you can press sliver with fingers.

Arthritic hands can be soothed at night by wearing plastic disposable gloves, type used by doctors. They cause hands to perspire; that is damp heat.

Ice cubes on burn and sprain, insect bite, even backache.

Shoes should be $1/2$ inch longer than your big toe. Feet swell in the afternoon, so get shoes then and measure right and left foot. One is bigger — fit it.

Soap powder is good for bites and infections. Soak. And good for varicose veins.

Vinegar on back of tongue will stop hiccups.

Use ear plugs when shooting shotgun.

Milkweed juice will remove warts.

Lanolin good for chapped hands.

If a bug gets in your ear, hold a light to your ear and it will come to the light.

Drink sweet milk after eating onions and drink black coffee after eating garlic.

Dandruff may be seborrhea caused by overactive sebaceous gland. Cut down on fats, chocolate, nuts, caffeine.

Use a solution of 2 tablespoons of soda, 1 quart water on sunburn that has blistered. Cover with a sterile dressing, soaked.

Hold ice on deep sliver and it won't hurt to remove.

Rub ice on tongue, and bitter medicine will be milder.

People at 60 years with type A blood have more fractures than in type O. Type B blood live longer than other types.

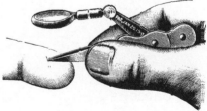

Remove tight ring with cold soapy water.

Cut end of porcupine quills and let out air, and
they can be pulled out by fingers.

A sliver can be drawn out with a poultice of sugar,
soap and water. Make a paste. For boils eat all
of raisins in one day.

People who think time heals everything haven't
tried sitting it out in a doctor's waiting room.

Grandpa's Kitchen

Sweeten coffee pots: use baking soda solution. On aluminum, use cream of tartar.

Add soda in water to wash greasy pans.

Place $1/2$ cup of ammonia in oven the night before [cleaning]. Burned-on grease will wash off in morning from fumes.

Boil beans without salt and add any meat the last twenty minutes. Beans will not be tough.

Rub olive oil in wood bowls and wipe next day.

Put lump sugar in refrigerator and leave for a few days. It will not be lumpy.

Do not cut root of onion and it will not smell. The odor is in the root. Also, will not make you cry.

Before squeezing oranges dip in hot water — also lemon and grapefruit. They will give more juice than cold.

Use two thimbles to grate with, save fingers.

Marinate pork chops in soy sauce flavored with
sugar, garlic and ginger, then broil. Make sure
pork is cooked good through.

If you need one or two servings of orange juice
each day, keep concentrate frozen, put a
tablespoon in each glass and add water.

When frying chicken, try dipping the pieces into
heavy cream before coating it with seasoned
flour.

When you make fudge, pour in small paper
cups — it will harden better.

Don't use detergent in your iron skillet. It will
remove the film of fat from pan and make it
rust.

Close refrigerator door on a newspaper. If it pulls
out easy, the door leaks.

When food is salted too much, stretch a wet cloth tight over pot, sprinkle white flour over the cloth, let stand for a few minutes to remove salt.

In broiling fish, use a piece of foil wider than fish, and when it is done on one side, use spatula and turn foil and fish same time and pull out foil and broil that side.

Put a dozen or more rice [grains] in bottom of salt and pepper shakers — will not get moist.

Rub Vaseline on bottom of ice tray. Will not stick in freezer.

If deep freeze stinks or refrigerator, put in charcoal in stocking or bowl, change after a while.

Parboil ducks with apples, and when they turn dark the fishy taste is gone.

Clorox will remove berry and
    walnut stains from hands.
    Then wash hands in soap
    and water.

Half of potato will clean kitchen
    knife.

Add a raw potato to over-salty
    soup, boil. Will remove some of the salt.

If coffee tastes bitter, as soon as you open can,
    put in freezer and it will keep fresh. Oil in
    coffee turns rancid, that is, bitter. It will not
    freeze.

Put corn plasters on bottom of appliances. Will
    not scratch.

Use lemon on food stains before water. Drop the
    lemon juice on, then use soapy water.

Dark pork is better than light, less loss in
    cooking.

Tomato catsup will clean copper.

Shape hamburger patties in large jar lid lined
with waxed paper. The paper releases them
from the lid.

To slice mushrooms, stick with fork and slice
through the tines.

Store apples with potatoes — they will not sprout.

Good steak sauce: catsup, worchestershire sauce,
a dash of tabasco to butter and heat.

To remove odor from refrigerator, place
3 tablespoons of vanilla extract in cup, lower
part of refrigerator for 2–3 hours.

To line drawers with paper, fold paper on top
inside, then turn it, the over-fold to the
bottom.

Rinse sauce pan with cold water before heating milk — prevents sticking.

To remove odor from refrigerator, use 1 lb. coffee, fresh-ground, in cloth bag. Also, soda in cup.

Use pipe cleaners to clean the tiny openings in the parts of your can opener.

Soak dry cheese in milk for freshness.

Rinse skillet in cold water before frying bacon, will not curl.

Store lettuce separately, as apples and other vegetables give off gas and rust.

A few cloves in the corners of your shelves in cupboards will discourage ants and give a spicely smell to your cabinets.

When boiling corn on the cob, add a cup of milk and teaspoon of sugar — tastes better.

A tiny sprinkling of cornmeal, if used on greased bread pans, will never become sticky from baked-on grease. The cornmeal absorbs all excess oil.

When a kitchen sink plugs, probably is grease. Pour a cupful of table salt and one of baking soda down the drain, followed by a pot of boiling water.

Put newspapers in sink when peeling potatoes or vegetables and lift out for garbage can.

A fresh egg sinks in water. The shell should be dull and rough. The yolk should be in the center. Hold egg to light, it should not shake loosely.

Stick toothpicks in onions and cabbage when boiling. They will not fall apart.

Scatter borax powder under shelf paper in cupboard in places where roaches hide. In a week you will be rid of them.

When defrosting refrigerator, put a handful of salt in water, hot — it will defrost twice as fast.

When mixing meatballs, put in plastic bag and knead. No greasy bowl to wash.

Thick catsup and worchestershire sauce and some horseradish. Mix — this is shrimp dip.

Use pretzel sticks to stick cheese squares and eat all.

Use nylon net to remove fish
scales.

Thirty minutes before cooking
steak, rub the two sides with
vinegar, you will find it
tender and juicier (no vinegar
flavor after).

Boiled beets pop right out of
their skins if dipped in cold
water after boiled.

Celery in cold water and
1 teaspoon of sugar, soak
one hour.

Cook roasts at 200 degrees; it takes long but will
taste better.

When brown sugar hardens, put in fruit jar with
a slice of white bread. Sugar will turn soft, and
bread will be hard.

Your pancakes will not stick if you rub pan with a
    salt bag instead of grease.

To broil meat over live coals, after coals have
    burned down, throw a handful of salt. It will
    deaden the smoke.

The color of the egg is the breed of the chicken.

When broiling meat, add salt just before serving;
    it will not draw the juices out.

Fresh eggs are rough,
    the smoother the
    shell and shiny, the
    older the egg.

A pinch of powdered
    sugar and one of
    cornstarch will
    prevent collapse of
    omelette; mix with
    eggs.

Coffee pot will keep sweet if salt is sprinkled
    inside and rubbed with damp cloth.

Use a rubber crutch tip on hammer head to beat
    out dents and put pans on sandbag.

Wrap cheese in cloth, dampen with vinegar, will
    not mold.

Fish odors from cooking
    utensils will vanish
    quickly if you add
    2–3 tablespoons of
    ammonia to the
    dishwater.

Wrap cloth wet with
    vinegar around bacon;
    it will not mold or
    taste bad.

To clean kitchen grease,
>   remove with trisodium phosphate.

Wrap a piece of charcoal in paper and place in
>   silver chest. Silver will not tarnish.

It is better to throw it out than throw it in.

Don't ever leave potatoes in the sun because this
>   causes chemical changes in the roots that are
>   harmful to humans.

Vanilla flavoring comes from a climbing orchid.

Catsup stains should be removed soon. Flush
>   with neutral detergent and water using a fairly
>   concentrated solution. Lubricate the rest of
>   the stain with glycerine. Flush again with
>   detergent and water.

Remove the stains in cups by rubbing with salt.

Use salt and grapefruit shell to clean copper.

Chocolate stains are easily removed with an application of glycerin. Rub it into fabric well and wash in plain water. If all is not removed, do it over again.

Grease, sugar, gravy or a combination of all — lay on a towel, dab on a detergent and water, rub gently, use enough water until the stain goes right through the bottom material.

Grandpa's Garden

Epsom salts are good for evergreens. Small amount — it is magnesium sulfate. Also give iron when they turn yellow.

For droopy house plants, soak empty eggshells in water and pour on plants.

Trimming fruit trees should be done in the winter, November 1 to March 15.

Transplant rhubarb in November.

Spray early in the morning.

Put slip of a rose in raw potato to start it.

Bake all soil used in house plants 180 to 240 degrees Fahrenheit 60 minutes. Use one-third sack of peat moss and heavy soil.

Use 1 tablespoon of detergent to 3 gallons of
water for fairy ring.

Small ants or army ants will not cross a line of
talcum powder.

Rabbits like apples and apple peelings and are
caught in traps with apples.

Baby oil will repel clover mites — a light coating
on window sill.

Divide and replant rhubarb in April when buds
first come out on it. Stalks should be 1 inch
wide, rich soil. Do not pick rhubarb for two
years after planted. Nitrogen and water in
spring. To freeze, just cut and put in plastic
bags. Cover new plants below 2 inches.

Put plastic bag over plants to hold moisture in
when going out.

To keep dogs away from flowers, put pepper on them.

Peonies require a great deal of water from the time the seeds begin to swell until the opening of the blossoms.

If you think a heavy frost is going to occur some night, you can spray the tree lightly with water in the evening, then thoroughly soak the ground area under the tree. As the water evaporates, it raises the temperature of the surrounding air, could save the blossoms.

Do not water grapes when in bloom; the pollen will fall without pollinating the grapes.

Tie rubber snake in nut trees — will keep squirrels and birds away.

Cucumber split lengthways — put where ants are. Also, sprinkle cinnamon where they walk, also sprinkle talcum powder — any should work.

Set shallow pans of beer to drown slugs. Beer attracts them. They are out at night. Also, lay boards flat and they will be under them in the daytime.

Grape leaves crinkle if any poison is around. Don't hurt them.

Pull sprinkler with rope and the hose to pull back the other way.

Peach borers: apply mothball crystals around the ground level of young tree and mound soil over this about 6 inches high. Use about $1/2$ to 1 ounce of crystals.

Put tomatoes that are green in plastic bag with an apple — very ripe. Punch a few holes in bag, keep at 70 degrees.

Banana peels are good for roses. Bury shallow
    around plant once a month.

Store apples with potatoes — they will not sprout.

Add 1/2 inch peat moss, 50% sand to low places
    in lawn, winter, spring.

Start seeds in grapefruit skins and set out skin
    and all. It will soon rot.

Onions will help to keep bugs away; plant with
    other plants, also chives and oregano.

Pinon nuts have a good crop every seven years.

Lady bugs will keep other bugs off vegetables.

Leaves and grass clippings and fruit parings
    make good fertilizer. Put in pile to rot, then
    spade in ground. Peat moss and hay and straw
    also. Salt and water will kill cabbage worms.
    Plain water on aphids.

A broom will work as a spray, put in water and
  shake.

Concord grapes, grape vines should be trimmed
  severely to produce much fruit.

Do not irrigate when plants are in bloom — you
  get more fruit.

Cut big coffee can's bottom
  out and put over tomato
  plants. This may be left
  on all season. No
  cutworms — or use paper
  cups.

Sew a pocket on each knee,
  insert a sponge in each
  pocket and you will have
  cushions as you work.

To keep wood from rotting, 4 parts sodium
fluoride and 25 parts water and saturate
wood.

Add an aspirin to cut flowers; they will stay fresh.
They will keep longer if you dip the cut tips in
boiling water.

An empty salt box is a good
container for bird seed.

Put salt on after cutting
bushes or trees, and root
will die.

If plants become pale, shine
a 100-watt bulb on them
for a couple of hours as
twilight sets in. Put bulb
close, but don't burn
them.

A few drops of lavender oil on cloth hung on
screen will keep flies away.

Watermelon and peach stains will remove with
pure glycerin. Leave on for a short time and
wash in clear water.

Bury a strip of tar paper in a trench about
6 inches deep. It will keep out other weeds and
grass. A layer of rock salt in driveway will keep
out grass under the gravel.

Cut flower stems at angle so when they rest on
bottom they can draw water and air. Cut daily.
Flowers heal on old cut. Remove all leaves
below water line.

I talk to my plants in the garden, but the weeds
have been listening in.

Poison flowers: mistletoe berries, poinsettia leaves, hyacinth blooms, narcissus blooms, buttercup, oleander — deadly, wisteria, jasmine — deadly, laurels, rosemary peas, lily of the valley, larkspur, daisies, bleeding hearts, rhododendron, azaleas, hemlock.

Apple seeds are poisonous, also peach and apricot seeds have cyanide. English ivy, sweet peas, iris, elephant ear, lantana, holly.

Science & History

When mice start leaving houses and fowl don't go
   to roost at sunset, and neighborhood dogs
   bark incessantly, look for an earthquake.

Zippers came out in men's pants in 1926.

More people die in March than any other month.
   Next is February and January, least in August.

Oil of mustard on body and feet will keep
   bloodhounds from trailing you.

To copy from a newspaper, use a piece of waxed
   paper over print and rub with a table knife. It
   will transfer on waxed paper. Lay it over on
   paper and transfer it same way, hold knife on
   a 45-degree angle (gentle pressure), do it to
   funny pictures.

If a dog chases a car, squirt ammonia with water
   pistol in his face.

A deer's eyes are green at night, and cow's and bear's eyes are red.

To pour heavy stuff out of jar, put in soda straw for air.

When lost, spider webs are on south side of ridge, goldenrod blooms bend to the north.

To charge old batteries, dissolve 1 ounce Epsom salt in warm water and add to each cell.

A man is as tall as from fingertip to fingertip with arms outstretched.

The Great Auk disappeared in June 1844.

The healthiest place in America is in Nebraska in the valley of the Big Blue and Little Blue rivers in the city of Lincoln. The death rate is only $1/2$ as high as in Augusta, Georgia.

To find water in the desert look for desert ants —
  they live where there is underground water.

Intense stress and terrifying experiences can
  cause diabetes.

Body temperature is highest at later afternoon or
  early evening, the lowest from 2–4 am.

The male is 5 pounds heavier, the female is
  5 pounds lighter than in 1912.

To take pictures of babies, give baby small piece
  of lemon; they like it. Also, put tape on their
  big toe or put his fingers in sugar. Or a baby
  hard to take a picture of — put baby in water.
  Tack up tablecloth for background, move in
  close, give small toys.

Tight shoes: wet inside with alcohol and wear
  until dry.

Grandpa's Gadgets

Place a penny into a tread groove so that Abe's head slips down into the slot. If you can see Lincoln's hairline, you need a tire.

Put wax on zipper for free travel.

Prevent splitting — clamp board bottom and top before driving nail in thin wood. Also, when sawing plywood.

Use rollers made of synthetic fibers for a nice paint job.

Use nylon net to clean false teeth.

To soften a chamois cloth, soak in warm water — a spoon of olive oil is added.

Fuzz balls on cloth can be removed with sandpaper.

Before paint, put on socks over shoes. Lay wet newspaper on floor near wall. Turn can upside down the night before to mix the paint.

Put some detergent in a bucket of hot water,
4 cups of Sal soda, take a long-handled sponge
mop and tie a small hand towel near the
sponge to keep the water from dripping down
your arms. As soon as the water is slightly
dirty change it so it will not streak the ceiling.

A cork inside of a bottle can be removed — pour
ammonia so cork will float, and then in several
days it will eat cork and so will come out of
bottle.

More heat will be reflected in room if you will affix
with thumb tacks aluminum foil behind
radiators.

Use striped denim for ironing board — use to line
up.

Move heavy furniture by putting flattened milk
cartons under.

Strain paint with nylon net. Boil old paint
   brushes in vinegar. If not clean, change
   vinegar and boil fifteen more minutes.

Put adhesive rubber on back of pictures.

To strain paint, cut screen to fit inside of can and
   let it settle to the bottom.

To repair sweater use knitted socks.

Clear plastic tape applied over the cutting
   guideline will keep veneer free of ragged edges
   and splinters when you undertake to saw it.

A mixture of ground cork and clear shellac will
   patch linoleum.

Hold mirror against wall for a few hours. If damp,
   it's ventilation that is needed.

If transparent tape gets hard, place on edge on
   wet sponge 10–15 minutes.

Use a bar of soap to pick up broken glass.

Use lipstick container for fish hooks; turn to bring up hook.

To remove tight cork from bottle, dip a woolen cloth in boiling water and wrap around the neck for a few minutes.

Disabled people getting out of bed — straight-back chair, cut legs off to fit under bed, shove under. You can hang things on back of chair.

Wax grooves in window if it sticks.

If drain pipe leaks, cover with wet plaster and cloth, tie it with a string and let it dry.

Paint cans in car will mix paint.

Use eyedropper for hard-to-oil places.

Use old distributor cap for pencil holder.

To paint nickel or other smooth surface paint with thinned shellac first. When painting around light fixtures, tie a paper bag or plastic around it. Use small can on handle of paintbrush or paper plate to keep paint from running down your hand. Paint luminous paint on top end of arrow and look for it after dark.

Fasten a meat grinder on iron board if no other place for it.

Use a button hook or old-fashioned hair pin to button top shirt button.

Put heavy aluminum foil over the ironing board, under cover. Heat reflected from foil helps in ironing.

Hang trousers by the waistband with clothes pins to hanger.

To tighten a hole in plaster, wrap cloth around it and put in glue. When glue hardens it will be tight.

Use ice cube to wet stamps and envelopes.

Use coarse sandpaper to iron pleats. Put under the pleats to hold in place.

Beeswax is best for zippers. Will not stain suspenders, falls off.

Shower curtain rings hold washers.

Put dishwashing soap around glass about 2 inches around woodwork to paint.

Burn end of rawhide laces lightly so they will harden and go into eye better.

A dime makes a good screwdriver.

Rubber hose wrapped on jar cover will help open.

Put bottle caps on bottom of shoes for nonskid.

Screws in plastic will hold; drive a nail first then
put in steel wool in hole and put in screw.

A screw that comes loose, put a drop of lacquer
on threads and screw in. Can be removed with
a screwdriver.

If car don't idle and everything has been done,
check motor bolts supports.

Dirty posts and ground cables can make car
lights dim when you slow down.

Shellac should be thinned 50% with denatured
alcohol to use. Wash brush in denatured
alcohol. Wait three hours for second coat.

Use a window shade to lay on when working
under car, then roll it back up.

Put zipper on string over shoulder to close.

Cut emery paper to sharpen scissors.

Don't throw out worn pillowcases. They make wonderful dust covers for clothing, hung in closets. Just snip a hole in the middle of the closed end and pull the hanger through.

Use salt bag to clean snow and ice from windshield.

Use rinsable paint remover on masonry walls, set for ten minutes, then wash off.

Use 6 sacks of cement to each cubic yard and 6 gallons of water to each sack.

To stain an unfinished picture, use paste shoe polish. Let it dry and then polish with a cloth.

Put Vaseline on hinges and doorknobs when painting doors.

Plastic pencil — small hairline cracks can be filled with spackling material. Dress and sand.

If your electric clock buzzes or whirs, try turning it upside down for several hours.

To make sure the buttons are placed where you want them, use a strip of cellophane to secure them on cloth. Pull off after.

Line your paint tray with aluminum foil that you can throw away later.

Soak neglected paintbrushes in hot vinegar to restore pliability — or Mr. Clean, 50%.

Chipped enamel — Get some epoxy enamel. It comes in two cans. Mix equal amounts. Apply immediately. Use an artist's paint brush — at least two coats to fill in level.

Paint lighter colors to make room look bigger, and
darker color will make the room look smaller.
Paint ceiling dark to lower it. Paint the far wall
on long narrow room dark to make it more
rectangular. Pick a color one shade lighter
than you want. Paint in a W pattern, then roll
up and down to blend in. Solvent brand paint
is best, but harder to clean up. Yellow and
pink are the hardest to cover up. Synthetic
brushes are best for latex, hog bristle best for
solvent paints like high-gloss enamels. Do not
stop painting in middle of wall.

Tie sponge to wrist when washing on a ladder.

Soak a cork in boiling water to make it bigger.

To drive nail into plaster wall, dip in melted
paraffin.

Window frosting, use 3 teaspoons Epsom salts to
a glass of water.

When painting with oil paint, put brushes in
plastic bag and freeze.

To make a house look taller, re-roof it with
brightly colored asphalt shingles that contrast
with the rest of the exterior. If a house seems
too tall, subdued-colored shingles will create
the impression of lowering the roof.

To fill small holes in linoleum, melt wax crayon of
same color and pour in holes.

String beads on dental floss; is strong as wire.

You can keep the lid of your
minnow bucket tightly closed
with the spring assembly from a
mousetrap hinge. Drill two holes
near the hinge of bucket lid and
insert the staples that hold
spring to mousehold. Bend end
inside.

Pencil clip holds screws.

To make a keyhole easier to find in the
dark, paint a $1/2$-inch stripe of luminous
paint all around it.

To remove lint from dark garments, use a
nylon net.

To kill flies at night, turn out light in house
and turn on outdoor light. Fly will set
on screen door.

If you have lost a clasp on beads, use hook and eye
and press the prongs together. Be sure to lace
the thread through both sides of the hook and
eye so that they will lie flat against the neck.

Wash hands in pure vinegar after working with
cement.

To cut straight line on things, use crack in table
leaf.

Sew rubber fruit jar rings on bottom of rugs that curl and slip.

Drilling holes through wood — Clamp another piece of wood on back side. Will not splinter hole.

For wood siding, use an oil-base paint. Use waterproof and masonry paint on masonry.

Wet a string before tying. It will not slip.

To paint bottom of door, use a toothbrush.

Use a small cake-decorating tube for a better job of applying putty. Warm the putty in warm water.

Drill small holes in hammer handle. It will not slip in hand. Small holes form vacuum.

A few drops of hydrogen peroxide will loosen the most tight screw, bolt or nut. Let it soak a few minutes.

Soak loose handles in engine oil a few hours to tighten.

A door that is tight on bottom, place a piece of rough sandpaper on bottom and open and close door.

Walls that are rough, use textured paint; it will cover a multitude of sins.

Window screens painted with white or aluminum paint thinner with turpentine will keep outsiders from seeing in but will not interfere with you seeing out.

Mix putty with paint of the color you want. This saves painting after they are puttied.

When you paint with a spray gun, hold the gun 6–10 inches from the object or wall. Move the gun across the surface with steady, even strokes, using a free-arm motion. Keep the gun perpendicular to and at an equal distance from the surface.

To paint screens, use a screen applicator available at paint stores.

Heat nails in hot water and they will not crack plaster.

Squeaky floor, pour liquid soap hot into cracks.

Cracks in stucco house, apply waterproof texture paint, will seal cracks or a mixture of portland cement and water to a paste. Put on with brush.

To remove old putty, use red-hot iron on it slow.

Put beeswax on screws.

Use auto jack to lift out old posts. Slip a chain over a hook on jack and loop around post and pull out.

To check for moisture in basement, fasten a piece of aluminum foil on wall with tape. If top is wet it is condensation. If inside it is seepage on floor, use rubber mat.

To saw plywood, put strip of cellophane tape on bottom and saw through, will not splinter.

Shellac drawers inside and out, and then they will not stick.

To lay out a curved driveway, use a hose and drive stakes to follow contour.

Drain unplugger — get old inner tube, cut out valve stem on a 6-inch-diameter circle of rubber. Attach a hand pump. Hold over drain tight. Have a friend pump.

If your shoe pinches, lay a cloth moistened in hot water over the spot, leave on for several minutes.

"Automatic" simply means that you cannot repair it yourself.

To keep roller skates from rusting, wrap in aluminum foil.

Money Management

In the pink is the way you feel when you get out of the red.

If a man stood over a big hole in the ground and dropped in a twenty-dollar bill every minute, day and night, it would take him ninety-five years to throw a billion dollars into the hole.

Inflation is when the buck doesn't stop anywhere.

Your debt should not exceed 35% of your pay.

If you think education is expensive, try ignorance.

Make it do or do without.

The large print giveth, and the small print taketh away.

If any should not work, neither should he eat.

People are still willing to do an honest day's work.
The trouble is they want a week's pay for it.

Crime wouldn't pay if the government ran it.

The shortest line in the world
is people who claim they
are overpaid.

There is a pot of gold at the
end of the rainbow —
which end?

I never saw an armored truck
follow a hearse to the
graveyard.

Money don't talk these days;
it goes without saying.

Money won't buy happiness but it helps you look for it in comfort.

Nowadays when a man looks after his money, he is saying goodbye to it.

Travels With Grandpa

List:

Get pills, Tums, checkbook, Maalox, glasses, case cleaner, blackberry compound, blackberry brandy, gum, Vaseline, boric acid salve, Kodak, razor, shave cream, toothpicks, nail file, polarized glasses, paper and pencil, toothbrush and paste, one roll toilet paper, candy mints, small screwdriver, socks, shirts, underwear, handkerchief. Bring warm coat, gloves, pencil and paper, phone book, soap box and towel, mirror.

Freeze water in milk cartons for trips. Also, as it thaws drink it or use as ice.

Clean bugs off the car with a solution of baking soda in water. Use a ball of aluminum foil dipped in water to clean small rust spots off bumpers and chrome.

Mildew on luggage — ammonia water and disinfectant and moth flakes or balls dissolve the mildew, odor also. Odor of mothballs is gone in fresh air.

Rub onion on car windshield, clean first, dry and rub after onion has been put on.

Make a packing list and paste inside suitcase, won't forget anything.

Wash dishes and put in mesh orange bag and hang in tree to dry when camping out.

A trip to the mountains:

Take 1 quart water, some food, a small first aid kit with large Band-Aids, a waterproof matchbox or lighter, a poncho and a whistle.

Skunk: if you get sprayed by a skunk, don't burn your clothes, simply wash in ammonia or chloride of lime and hang them out in the breeze. Soaking clothes in tomato juice for six hours also does the trick. To de-skunk your skin, use carbolic soap and warm water. Wiping eyes with [plain] water will speed their recovery. Tears will do it in about twenty minutes. The scalp is the hardest part of the body to de-skunk. Usually, a Yul Brynner haircut will do it.

Put soap on bottom of camping frying pan, soot will wash off.

Good maps tell a motorist everything he wants to know except how to fold them up again.

Carry soaped wash cloth in plastic bag. Also a wet one to clean up the soap later.

You can carry a TV dinner while hunting and when hungry heat over campfire.

Put bug spray on table legs when in hills to keep them off.

Boil egg in plastic bag. Tie bag. Let string hang. That is, egg without shell.

After airing an overnight bag, put in a cake of soap before storing it. This eliminates the stale, musty odor.

To discourage ants, put small piece of blotting paper saturated with insect repellent under each leg of a picnic table.

To remove musty odor from inside of trunk, crush up newspaper and put inside. Leave two or three weeks, see top is tight.

To heat sandwiches, put aluminum foil on and put on hot motor.

Carry a salt shaker filled with cream of tartar and sprinkle on windshield to remove greasy film in rain. Use wipers or use a cloth.

Leather shoes can be weatherproofed — use ski wax, apply hot, rub with stiff brush. After, rub with cloth.

Dip matches in paraffin from old candle, and in wet weather they will light.

Cottonwood buds just starting to open are good trout bait.

Piano stools are good for duck blind; will turn any way.

Use hubcap to bring water to car, also use a shovel.

Vaseline between toes for long walks, and woolen socks help keep feet okay.

Vaseline on face and ears keeps off sunburn.

In an underdeveloped country don't drink the water — in a developed country don't breathe the air.

Drive carefully. Remember, it's not only a car that can be recalled by its maker.

Hang a shower curtain on a Hula Hoop to a tree with metal hooks and slip them on the hoop — instant privacy.

Put a damp cloth in plastic bag and use after fishing.

A fishing rod is stick with a hook at one end and
a fool at the other.

Emergency sinkers — use toothpaste tubes,
shaving soap tubes, cut tubes with scissors.

Grandpa's Spring Cleaning Tips

Cut slices of onions in pail of water and leave in room to remove odors of paint.

Rub oil stain with lard, let set at least one hour, then wash. Or use shampoo on oil stain and let set one hour and wash.

To wash gloves, leather except chamois, use soapsuds, keep gloves on hands.

Steel wool will not rust in a jar of soda water.

Rings on furniture — we rub Vaseline, toothpaste and oily nut meats.

Soak shower head in vinegar when clogged.

Rubber eraser will clean coins.

To soften a chamois cloth, soak in warm water — a spoon of olive oil is added.

Shiny pants — rub white vinegar with terry cloth and let dry.

Put shampoo on dirty shirt collars.

Window cleaners will clean straw hats.

Heat marks from furniture — use camphor or peppermint oil. Lemon juice will remove rust stains. Then hold spot over teakettle.

Cleaning ceilings: put some detergent in a bucket of hot water, 4 cups of Sal soda, take a long-handled sponge mop and tie a small hand towel near the sponge to keep the water from dripping down your arms. As soon as the water is slightly dirty change it so it will not streak the ceiling.

Try mayonnaise on scratches — leave it set, remove and rub hard with soft rags; it will look as good a new.

White spots on furniture: sponge with turpentine and put on fresh wax after.

Yellowed lace can be bleached by soaking in sour milk.

Alcohol will remove hair spray.

Use alcohol to remove ballpoint ink.

Put liquid starch on grease stains on wallpaper. Let dry and brush off. More than once if necessary.

Use cold water to remove something that spills on cloth — cold, not hot.

Bathroom glass will not fog up if wiped with canned shaving cream. Also works on glasses.

Cloves packed with woolens keep out mice and moths.

Damp coffee grounds and squeeze lemon juice
over grounds — will wash grime and stains
from hands.

Equal parts of cream of tartar and salt will
remove rust stains from fabric. Wet the spots
and spread mixture on thickly, then put it in
sun.

Rub white vinegar on mark left on dresses when
hem is lowered, then press with warm iron.

To clean grease from hands like mechanics, use
$1/2$ pint of cylinder oil, wash till all grease is
dissolved, wipe with towel, finish with warm
water and soap. Also, when greasy hands are
washed, after use sugar on hands — will clean
them.

Cigar ash can rub out that table ring. Use with
salad oil or varnish. Use oil of camphor.
Final — use FFF powdered pumice. Damp with
paraffin oil; small scratches use iodine. Dent
in wood, place a damp cloth over it, lay a coin
on top and heat with torch or solder iron. To
clean kitchen grease remove with trisodium
phosphate.

Toothpaste will clean silver.

Yellow stain from bathtub — use three parts of
cream of tartar and one part of peroxide.
Make and spread on and
let dry and wipe off.

Club soda will remove carpet
stains when not too old,
will not mark or [leave]
rings.

Dig your fingernails in soap before a dirty job and they will clean easier.

If mildew forms on enameled walls wash the walls in a solution of 1.5 cups of household bleach to a gallon of water. Brush this on the affected areas and let it remain for five minutes, then rinse with clean water. Remove mildew by washing the garments in hot suds, moistening it with lemon juice and salt and letting it dry in the sun. If the stain is old, bleach with hydrogen peroxide; be sure to rinse well.

Rub toothpaste on stain or ring in bathtub, then wash after fifteen minutes.

Alcohol will rinse mustard stains.

Make a paste of cream of tartar and peroxide and apply with stiff brush on rusty bathtub.

If floor creaks, fill the cracks with talcum powder, then shellac the floor.

Rust stains on leaky faucets — use vinegar-soaked cloth, rinse and dry.

Baking soda and water will remove labels and stamps also.

Starch, Faultless, 1 quart to gallon water, wash windows.

To dull a shiny coat collar, sponge over with a cloth dipped in hot vinegar, press while damp on wrong side.

Iron shirt collar on wrong side first.

When suds disappear, add more soap — it is a sign the soap is loaded with dirt.

Costume jewelry will not tarnish if you put in a piece of blackboard chalk.

Strip newspaper and wet it and lay on dusty floor; it will peel up dust.

Remove grease stains, kitchen floor or cement steps. Use baking soda, brush back and forth, repeat if necessary.

To clean white plastic, use dental cream, use with damp cloth.

A pinch of cream of tartar in wash will whiten clothes that have turned yellow.

You can get a better crease when pressing pants by using a damp cloth, then before cloth is dry, replace it with a sheet of heavy wrapping paper and go over crease again. If bottom of iron gets a buildup of starch, remove it by rubbing over salt sprinkled on brown paper. When dacron or nylon sweaters have stains at collars and cuffs, [rub] shampoo into the fabric; it will cut grease and leave clean, rinse well.

Marked woodwork, walls and floor colored with crayon can be removed with ammonia.

Vinegar and soda will clean chrome.

A solution of pine oil cleaner in washer will remove tar and dirt from sneakers and gym clothes.

Nylon turned yellow is a buildup of detergent, wash complete cycle in clear water. You may have to repeat but it will come back to its original whiteness.

Polish brass with water that onions have been boiled in; it will be tarnish-free.

Use peanut butter oil to polish chrome.

To get rid of alcohol spots on an oak floor, rub the spots with a cloth dampened with ammonia or a cloth treated with wax silver polish and boiled linseed oil.

To wash windows use a newspaper dipped in vinegar, wring out and wash windows.

Use coarse sandpaper to iron pleats. Put under the pleats to hold in place.

Baking soda will remove coffee stains.

You can prepare a good stain remover by mixing 1 quart of laundry bleach, 3 quarts water, 3 ounces trisodium phosphate and 1 ounce of laundry detergent.

If mildew is not removed before painting it will come through the new paint.

Use toothpaste to remove crayon marks on stucco house. [Scrub] with old toothbrush and wash with hose.

Mildew stains can be removed — soak pieces in buttermilk, move about so liquid reaches all spots. Soak until spots have disappeared. Rinse thoroughly in cold water, then wash.

To remove ink from cloth, soak in sour milk overnight, then wash garment.

Chalk will remove oil and dark spots from rug and other things. Rub on and leave until oil is removed — get soft chalk.

Wood that has dents in it, sand and put in boiling water.

Iodine stains on clothes — sponge with ammonia and then wash.

If color fabrics bleed, soak in strong salt water, cold for hour or more.

To clean marble stain, ammonia will remove most stains. Old ones will use powdered whiting. Get at paint store. Make a paste with acetone and leave for a few hours, keep it moist with acetone. Also, paste with peroxide and whiting after wash and polish marble.

Put open box of baking soda to keep out odors, good for two months, then put down kitchen sink.

Lemon juice and salt and lay on grass in sun to remove rust stains if wet. Also, boil in cream of tartar and water.

Household bleach will remove green fungus in birdcage. Put in newspaper and pour on bleach. Leave 15–20 minutes, remove and wash cage.

Furniture damaged by cigarette burns — fill the holes with beeswax and polish over with furniture polish.

A scorched iron bottom can be cleaned by using white vinegar and a cloth with a little rubbing.

Ballpoint ink can be removed with hairspray like mahogany wood.

To clean bronze use lemon juice and cigarette ashes.

Mercurochrome stains on rug — use effervescent denture tablets in one cup of hot water. Also, old blood stains.

Use black polish on driftwood. Also, spray gold or aluminum paint.

Denatured alcohol cleans pewter and nickel.

Some grease spots and oil can be removed with cornstarch. Cover spots, in one hour sweep away.

Mothballs will keep cats away.

Jewelry clean — $1/4$ cup ammonia, $1/4$ cup white vinegar, $1/8$ cup dishwashing detergent. Use brush, after soak and dip in clear water. Or toothpaste brush inside and out, rinse with warm water, or soak in solution of denture cleaning tablets and rinse.

To remove decals from wall dip a cotton ball in boiling hot vinegar and sponge the decal with it, sponge then wash it away.

To remove the fold wrinkles from a new no-iron shirt, put in dry into the dryer with a load of damp towels. Every wrinkle will fall out.

Substitute paste floor wax to shine your shoes.

Nail polish remover will remove tape — masking and other tape — from glass and wood.

Glue can be softened by a few drops of vinegar, shaking well.

Rub ice on wax, and it will harden to remove from rug.

Boil soda and water, then dip steel wool in, and it will shine brass.

Use garden sprayer — fill with hot mixture of water combined with 3 tablespoons of suds-less detergent and an equal amount of Sal Soda. Spray in a fine mist and will loosen wallpaper.

Remove fat or grease from cloth. Lay the garment on a flat surface, put paper toweling on bottom. Put baby powder on stain. Rub in stain with circular motion, let remain about fifteen minutes, then scrape with dull-edge knife.

Pure lemon extract will remove ink-stamped products.

Plastic pencil — small hairline cracks can be filled with spackling material. Dress and sand.

If heavy furniture has made deep dents in your carpeting, place a damp cloth over dent and press with a fairly hot iron. To raise the nap, finish with a gentle brushing with stiff brush.

To remove oil spots from wallpaper, if they are fresh, put on talcum powder and allow the paper to absorb it. Repeat if necessary.

A few drops of turpentine will soften shoe polish when hard.

Spots on stainless steel sinks disappear when rubbed with cloth that has a little vinegar in it.

Silver polish: Dissolve $1^1/2$ cups of soap flakes in $1^1/2$ cups of hot water. Cool, then add $^1/4$ lb. of whiting powdered calcium carbonate and 1 tsp. of ammonia. Store in tight jar.

Apply baking soda on cloth and dampen. Will remove bugs and grease from car windshield and grille.

A bowl of vinegar will help clear smoke in a room.

Lighter fluid will remove sticky glue from labels.

Vinegar will remove water stains.

Aluminum foil will scrub off rust on bumpers.

Pencil eraser will remove marks on piano keys.

Remove grease spots on rugs, apply baking soda, rub in well and let stand overnight. Electric sweeper will suck it up.

Wash windows cross-ways on one side and length-wise on the other side.

Wax inside of ash trays; ashes won't stick.

Scratch on the back of a mirror will not be visible from the front if you smooth aluminum foil over the area and secure it with shellac.

Use a solution of 2 tablespoons of soda, 1 quart water on sunburn that has blistered. Cover with a sterile dressing, soaked.

When you scorch a piece of cloth, rub some onion on it and leave for a short time. Then soak it in cold water and the mark fades.

Paste floor wax will remove the marks from woodwork caused by crayons.

Dirt and tar on hands — rub with Vaseline well and wipe with paper towel. Use same if tar on clothes, rub in and put in washer.

Oil and grease on brown or tan shoes can be removed by lemon juice.

Ammonia sprayed will keep out skunks.

To clean grease or engine oil from clothes, use a liquid rug cleaner. Soak entire garment in half water and half liquid for ten minutes — will come out clean.

Nylon and dacron — use window spray cleaner, rub until spots disappear.

To remove hairs from upholstery, use damp sand-paper.

To remove lipstick, rub the cloth with Vaseline or glycerin and then wash as usual.

Perspiration stains: remove by applying thick paste of baking soda, leave on fifteen minutes, then rinse out all paste.

Dent in wood — place a damp cloth over it, lay a coin on top and heat with torch or solder iron.

Words
to Live By

Anger is one letter away from danger.

Speak when you are angry, and you'll make the best speech you will ever regret.

If you don't say it, they can't repeat it.

Love is one set of glands calling to another.

Do not twist electric wires.

Man staggers through life yapped at by his reason, shoved by his appetites, whispered to by his fears, beckoned by his hopes.

Did is a word of achievement, won't is a word of retreat, might is a word of bereavement, can't is a word of defeat. Ought is a word of duty, try is a word of each hour, will is a word of beauty, can is a word of power.

Victory has many fathers; defeat is an orphan.

As soon as you replace a lost article you will find it.

No matter how well a toupee blends in the back, it always looks like hell in front.

Go to friends for advice, to women for pity, to relatives for nothing.

Pride gets no pleasure out of having something; only out of having more of it than the next man.

In a fight between you and the world, back the world.

Never leave hold of what you've got until you've got hold of something else.

If it happens, it must be possible.

When you get mountain sickness, go lower.

Integrity is keeping promises. Wisdom is not making such promises.

Even churches have rats in their basements.

A man is judged from his neck up, not his neck down.

Seek not every quality in one individual.

Other planets may not be able to support life, but it is not easy on this one either.

The hardest thing to learn in life is which bridge to cross and which to burn.

The more patience I have, the more people use it.

Late-night TV is educational. It usually teaches that you should have gone to bed earlier.

One way to stop a runaway horse is to bet on him.

One battle you don't mind losing is when you are fighting temptation.

Youth looks for greener pastures. Middle age is when we can hardly mow the one we've got.

People who tell you "don't let little things bother you" have never tried to sleep with a mosquito in the room.

Live so that you wouldn't be ashamed to sell the family parrot to the town gossip.

We are here to help others. What are the others here for?

Strike now or you will get the neck of the chicken and the rumble-seat ride.

Some people leave without saying goodbye, while others say goodbye without leaving.

Time heals all wounds, but time-and-a-half heals faster.

Smart is when you believe only half of what you hear. Brilliant is when you know which half to believe.

One who never asks knows either everything or nothing.

Education kills by degrees.

We live off a quarter of all we eat; doctors live off the other three-quarters.

Habit is like a soft bed — easy to get into but hard to get out of.

Physicians say the only way to keep your health is to eat what you don't want, drink what you don't like, and do what you'd druther not.

There is nothing wrong with having nothing to
 say unless you insist on saying it.

Love's first cousin is trust.

If at first you don't succeed, you are running
 about average.

Everyone needs a little nothing in their lives now
 and then.

Anyone who angers you conquers you.

A wife is someone who sits up with her husband
 when he is sick and puts up with him when he
 isn't.

There is a bigger fool than the fellow who knows it
 all; it is the fellow who will argue with him.

"That is a good question," usually means you get
 a lousy answer.

A person who says he is willing to meet you half way is a poor judge of distance.

How a man plays the game shows something of his character. How he loses shows all of it.

Never insult an alligator until you have crossed the river.

Beware of the half truth; you may have hold of the wrong half.

A neurotic builds castles in the air, a psychotic lives in them, the psychiatrist collects the rent.

He who cannot forgive others destroys the bridge which he himself must cross.

If you feel far from God, guess who moved.

The coating of civilization is so thin that it comes off with a little alcohol.

Keep a secret and it's your slave; tell it and it's your master.

The cheapest and most dependable labor-saving device is Mother.

An optimist is one who has two acorns and buys a hammock.

Worry is today's mouse eating tomorrow's cheese.

What does cheese say when it has its picture taken?

When you return to your boyhood town, you find it wasn't the town you longed for; it was your boyhood.